SHORT-TERM RENTAL MARKET

How to Create a Money Business!

Revit MONNE

Disclaimer Notice:

CONTENT

RENTAL-SHORT TERM MARKET 1

HOW TO CREATE A MONEY BUSINESS! 1

REVIT MONNE 1

INTRODUCTION 6

CHAPTER 1 12

REVIEW YOUR ADVERTISEMENT RESULTS. HOW
MANY PEOPLE RESPONDED TO YOUR ADS? 12

CHAPTER 3 34

ARE SHORT TERM RENTALS PROFITABLE? 34

CHAPTER 4 40

THE MOST SIGNIFICANT SHORT-TERM RENTAL
TRENDS OF 2023 40

CHAPTER 5 50

WHERE IS THE BEST SHORT-TERM RENTAL
LOCATION 50

MARKET FOR REAL ESTATE INVESTORS? 50

CHAPTER 6 64

DETERMINE PRICING 64

CHAPTER 7 78

7 BEST CITIES IN THE UNITED STATES FOR
SHORT-TERM RENTALS 78

2. THE CITY OF WASHINGTON, D.C. 82

3. SEATTLE, WASHINGTON 86

REFERENCES 103

INTRODUCTION

Are you looking for a new opportunity in the short-term rental market?

Airbnb might be just what you are looking for! here, we will discuss how to get started with Airbnb and learn about the booking process. We will also explore some of the benefits of using Airbnb as a short-term rental platform.

.7 Simple But Effective Ways to Drive More Traffic to Your Short-Term Rental Property

If you're looking to drive more traffic to your short-term rental property, you're in luck. In this blog post, we will discuss seven simple but effective ways that you can use to bring more people to your listing. Keep in mind that it's important to tailor these strategies to your specific business and target market. So let's get started!

1. Create a Professional Looking Website:

Today's digital world is all about presentation and having an aesthetically pleasing website for your short-term rental property can go a long way in helping you attract more customers. Make sure that your site is easy to navigate and has information on pricing, amenities, and pictures of the property that potential customers can view easily.

2. Utilize Social Media Marketing: Having active social media accounts with quality content can help drive traffic to your listing. Share photos of your rental and create engaging posts relevant to your target market to increase brand awareness and visibility online.

3. List Your Property on Multiple Platforms: By making sure that your property is listed on multiple platforms such as Airbnb and Flipkey, you can increase your chances of getting more bookings. Make sure to include all the relevant details about the rental in each listing and set up automatic notifications for when a booking is made.

4. Include Accurate Photos: Visuals are powerful and having accurate photos of your property can help potential customers make informed decisions faster. Take some time to take professional quality images of your rental that accurately showcase the features and amenities that it offers.

5. Make Sure That Your Property Has Good Reviews: Positive reviews from guests can help you attract more customers to your short-term rental property, so make sure that the experience you provide is professional and enjoyable. Ensure that your customer service is top-notch and ask past guests to leave a review after their stay.

6. Offer Incentives for Loyal Customers: Consider offering discounts or other incentives for loyal customers who frequently book with you. This will give them an incentive to come back again and can also attract new customers who may be on the fence about booking with you.

7. Invest in Good Quality Furnishings: Quality furnishings are essential for any short-term rental property as they help create a comfortable and inviting atmosphere for guests. Investing in good quality furniture and appliances can help you stand out from the competition as well as add value to your property.

By utilizing these seven simple but effective strategies, you can start driving more traffic to your short-term rental property quickly and easily. Keep in mind that it's important to tailor each strategy specifically to your business so that they are most effective at reaching your target market.

Good luck!

CHAPTER1
Review your advertisement results. How many people responded to your ads?

After placing ads for passive income opportunities

related to our short-term rental opportunity, we

were pleasantly surprised at the amount of

responses. We found that over a hundred

individuals showed interest in what we had to offer

and were eager to learn more about how this

could help them make passive income. This

enabled us to find the right people for the job and led to a very successful project launch.

What strategies do you use to market your short-term rental property?

We employ a number of effective strategies for marketing our short-term rental property. These include creating an attractive website and utilizing social media marketing, listing on multiple platforms, including accurate photos, using positive reviews from guests as leverage, offering incentives for loyal customers, and investing in top quality furnishings. Together these strategies help us build brand awareness, increase visibility online and generate more bookings for our rental property.

How can you make sure the customer experience is enjoyable?

Providing excellent customer service is essential to ensure that guests have a pleasant stay at our rental property. We focus on being available and responsive to any questions or concerns that our customers might have. Additionally, we strive to go the extra mile by providing personalized touches such as a welcome basket with snacks and beverages, as well as clean and comfortable accommodations. These little extras create an inviting atmosphere for guests and help ensure a pleasant experience.

What tips do you have for other owners of short-term rental properties?

My advice to other owners of short-term rentals is to be committed to providing excellent service and creating high quality experiences for their customers. Invest in good quality furniture and appliances, list your property on multiple platforms, include accurate photos, make sure that your property has positive reviews from guests, offer incentives for loyal customers, and use social media marketing to increase visibility. With these strategies, you will be able to stand out from the competition and generate more bookings for your rental property.

How do I start a short-term rental?

Starting a short-term rental can be a savvy decision to increase your income potential. It begins by doing the necessary research and familiarizing yourself with any local laws or government regulations. Once you have determined those requirements, it's time to begin advertising your rental space. Creating an attractive and informative listing helps prospective visitors understand exactly what is offered and sets expectations for their stay. Pricing must also be considered carefully; setting too high of prices wastes potential business whereas setting too low prices won't bring in adequate returns on investment. Maintaining an updated communication channel with guests will also help ensure that a positive experience leads to future bookings for investors looking to make money through short-term rentals.

What kind of insurance do I need for a short-term rental business?

When you're running a short-term rental business, it's important to have the right insurance in place to protect both yourself and your guests.

Depending on where you are located, there may

be certain requirements that you must fulfill in

order to legally rent out your property.

Additionally, some types of insurance can provide

additional peace of mind should something go

wrong during the course of a stay. Generally

speaking, the most basic form of insurance for

short-term rentals is liability coverage which will

protect you from any claims made by guests or

visitors who were injured while at your property.

You might also consider adding other forms like

property damage protection if necessary.

By having the right insurance, you can ensure that your business is covered should any issues arise.

How do I market my short-term rental listing?

Once you have found the perfect property for your short-term rental business and set up all the necessary insurance policies, it's time to start marketing your listing. The first step is to create a detailed description of your property that highlights its features and amenities. It's also important to include plenty of high quality photos so potential guests can get an idea of what they're booking. Next, you'll want to list your property on sites like Airbnb, Booking.com or VRBO where people can easily find it by searching for rentals in their destination city. Finally, you can also use social media to promote your listing and reach even more potential guests.

By following these steps, you should have everything you need to start attracting guests to your short-term rental business!

What are some tips for running a successful short-term rental business? Running a successful short-term rental business requires a lot of planning and preparation. Here are some helpful tips for ensuring that your venture is as profitable as possible:

• Set competitive rates – Be sure to check out what other properties in the area are charging so that you can stay competitive.

• Invest in high quality furnishings and amenities – Investing in comfortable furniture and luxurious amenities will help attract more guests and garner better reviews.• Offer promotions – Consider offering discounts or other promotions to entice potential guests to book with you.

• Respond promptly – Make sure to respond quickly to any inquiries or requests from potential guests so that they know their needs are being taken care of.

• Provide excellent customer service – It's important to provide friendly, helpful service in order for guests to have a pleasant experience at your property.

By following these tips, you can ensure that your short-term rental business is successful and profitable!

What kind of taxes do I need to pay for my short-term rental business?

When running a short-term rental business, you will be required to pay taxes on your income. Depending on where you are located, the specific tax requirements may vary. Generally speaking, most jurisdictions will require you to collect and remit occupancy taxes from guests as well as pay any applicable state and local taxes. Additionally, if your rental is classified as an investment property then you may also have to report it on your annual income tax return and pay additional taxes on the profits. It's important to research the specific taxation laws in your area before starting a short-term rental business so that you can stay compliant with all of the regulations. These are some of the taxes you may need to pay when running a short-term rental business. It's important to be aware of all applicable laws and regulations so that you can stay compliant and avoid any potential penalties.

What other services should I consider offering?

In addition to providing comfortable accommodations, there are many other services that you can offer to guests in order to give them an even better experience. For example, you could provide optional breakfast or airport pickup for an additional fee. You could also offer discounts on activities like boat tours or museum visits if they book multiple nights at your property. Additionally, offering laundry services and grocery delivery will make your rental more attractive for longer stays.

By offering these additional services, you can provide your guests with even more value and make their stay as comfortable and convenient as possible.

These are just some of the services that you could consider offering in order to create a better experience for your short-term rental guests. With a little bit of creativity, you can come up with even more ideas that will help differentiate your property from the competition!

By following these steps, you should be well on your way to running a successful and profitable short-term rental business. With the right combination of marketing, customer service, and additional services, you can attract more guests and provide them with an unforgettable experience.

What kind of insurance should I consider for my short-term rental business?

When running a short-term rental business, it's important to have the right kind of insurance in order to protect your property and guests from any potential liabilities. Depending on your specific situation, you may want to purchase some form of liability insurance or even property damage coverage. Additionally, many jurisdictions require hosts to carry workers' compensation insurance if they are hiring employees or contractors for their business.

It's also recommended that you carry a homeowners or landlords' policy that includes personal and commercial liability coverage, in case someone gets injured while staying at your property. While this type of insurance won't cover any damage caused by guests, it will help protect you from any potential lawsuits resulting from accidents or injuries.

By having the right kind of insurance in place, you can ensure that your rental business is protected in the event of any unexpected liabilities. Make sure to research all of the options available for your specific area and speak with an insurance professional before making a decision.

These are some important tips to consider when starting a short-term rental business. From marketing and customer service to taxes and insurance, there are many different things you need to be aware of in order to ensure success. With careful planning and preparation, you can create a successful short-term rental property that provides guests with an unforgettable experience!

Are there any other tips for running a successful short-term rental business?

Yes, there are many additional tips to consider when running a successful short-term rental business. First and foremost, it's important to offer excellent customer service in order to make sure that your guests have an enjoyable stay. Taking the time to respond promptly to inquiries and requests will help create a positive reputation and keep customers coming back. Additionally, it's a good idea to host regular events or activities on the property as this will give guests something extra to look forward to during their stay. You can also provide local recommendations of restaurants, shops, and attractions so that they have more ideas for things to do during their stay.

Finally, it's important to keep up with the latest trends in the industry and look for new ways to improve your rental business. Keeping a close eye on customer feedback and adjusting your services accordingly can help you provide better value and stay ahead of the competition. With these tips in mind, you should be able to run a successful short-term rental business!

These are just some of the tips that will help you create a successful short-term rental business. By following these steps and staying up to date with industry trends, you can ensure that your property stands out from the competition and provides guests with an unforgettable experience!

What should I do if I need help managing my short-term rental business?

If you find yourself needing help managing your short-term rental business, there are several options available to you. Many hosts choose to hire a property manager who can take care of the day-to-day tasks related to running the business, such as marketing and customer service.

Additionally, there are many software platforms that provide tools for landlords and property managers that can make your job easier. Finally, if you're looking for more comprehensive assistance, consider hiring a consultant or virtual assistant who specializes in the short-term rental industry. They can provide valuable insights and advice on how to get the most out of your business.

With these resources at your disposal, you should be able to effectively manage your short-term rental business. These are just some of the ways that you can get help managing your short-term rental business. With the right tools and support, you can ensure that your business is successful and provides guests with an unforgettable experience!

CHAPTER 3
Are short term rentals profitable?

Are you thinking of becoming a short-term rental property owner? Perhaps you've seen the potential for profit in news stories or friends' Facebook posts and want to get in on the action. Before you sign on the dotted line, though, it's important to understand exactly how profitable short-term rentals can be. In this post, we'll break down the numbers so you can decide if a short-term rental property is right for you.

The primary benefit of short-term rentals is that they can generate much higher rates than long-term leases. You may be able to charge hundreds or even thousands of dollars per week, depending on the location and amenities offered. Plus, you don't have to commit to a lease for an entire year, which means more flexibility. However, there are drawbacks to consider as well. For one thing, managing turnover from tenant to tenant can be time consuming and difficult. You'll also need to invest in furniture and other items for every unit in order to make it attractive enough for renters. Plus, you may need additional insurance coverage depending on the type of property you're renting out.Finally, there's no guarantee that your property will be profitable. It all depends on the local market and how much demand there is for short-term rentals in your area. If you do decide to invest in a short-term rental, it's important to research the area thoroughly before taking the plunge.Overall, short term rentals can be quite profitable when done right. While there are some risks involved, the potential rewards can far outweigh any initial investment. If you're interested in dipping your toes into this form of real estate investing, be sure to do your research and have a thorough understanding of what's involved before making any decisions. With a little bit of effort and planning, you may find that a short-term rental property is an excellent way to get started some of the challenges of starting a short-term rental business ARE

There are a few tips and tricks you can employ to make your short-term rental a success.

- 1. Make sure that you have all the necessary permits and licenses from local authorities before starting your rental business. This will ensure that you stay compliant with all applicable laws and regulations.

- 2. Take the time to thoroughly inspect the property and make sure that it is safe and in good condition before allowing any guests to stay.

- 3. Invest in a reliable security system to protect both you and your guests, as well as the property itself.

- 4. Consider offering amenities like free Wi-Fi access, cable TV, parking space, etc. to attract more guests.

- 5. Keep the property clean and tidy at all times and provide basic amenities like towels, toiletries, linen, etc. for your guests' convenience.

- 6. Advertise your short-term rental in multiple platforms like social media, classified websites and even on local business directories to get more bookings.

- 7. Make sure that you are well versed in the local laws and regulations related to short-term rentals so you can comply with them without any issues.

- 8. Provide a detailed list of rules and regulations for your guests so they know what is expected of them while staying at your property.

By following these tips and tricks, you can make sure that your short-term rental is a success.

CHAPTER 4
The most significant short-term rental trends of 2023

will be the ever-growing desire for convenience and personalization. Consumers will expect to have access to a wide range of services tailored to their individual needs, including intuitive check-in, efficient property management systems, smart home technology, personalized pricing structures, and more. With the emergence of short-term rental Marketplaces such as Airbnb and Vrbo, travelers will be able to find a wide range of rental options and prices. Furthermore, advances in artificial intelligence will allow for more tailored recommendations so that customers can find the perfect property for their stay quickly and easily.

Another trend to watch out for is local experiences. As travelers become increasingly interested in exploring different cultures and communities, short-term rental companies will have to adapt and offer personalized experiences. This could include curated tours, local cuisine delivery service, or even access to unique activities or events.

Finally, the sustainability of short-term rentals will become increasingly important in 2022. Consumers are starting to become more conscious about their carbon footprint and looking for ways to reduce it. As a result, rental companies will need to take steps to ensure their operations are environmentally friendly by minimizing energy consumption and water usage through efficient lighting and plumbing solutions. Companies should also look into green initiatives such as using renewable energy sources or investing in green building materials. The goal of going green is not only to reduce emissions but also to provide customers with a more enjoyable and responsible stay.

Overall, 2023 promises to be an exciting year for short-term rentals as the industry continues to evolve and adapt to consumer needs. With new technological tools, more sustainable operations, and personalized experiences being offered, this could well be a defining year for short-term rental trends. It will be interesting to see how these trends continue to shape and define the industry.

  With any luck, they will lead to an even more streamlined and enjoyable rental experience for customers.

And as the short-term rental sector continues to grow and evolve in 2023, it's likely that we'll also see newer approaches to managing rentals such as digital marketing, data analytics, automated payment processing and remote access. These advances will pave the way for a more modern and efficient rental experience, as well as give property managers more control over their properties and guest interactions. It's clear that 2023 promises to be an exciting year for short-term rentals with many new trends emerging. Consumers will have access to better rental options, personalized experiences, more sustainable operations and smarter technology. It will be interesting to see how these trends continue to shape the industry in the coming years.

As companies are always looking for new ways to stay ahead of the competition, it's likely that 3will bring a variety of new innovations and advancements to short-term rentals. It's an exciting time to be in the industry, and we can't wait to see what the future holds.

With all these trends on the horizon, it looks like 2022 is set to be a defining year for short-term rentals. We can only hope that these trends will help streamline and improve the rental experience for customers, while also allowing property managers to better manage their properties. We look forward to seeing what the future holds for the industry!

How do you analyze short-term rental properties?

Analyzing short-term rental properties requires a certain eye for financial opportunity. It is essential to think about the money associated with the property and how it can be put to work. Potential investors should look at factors such as what kind of return on investment is expected, any potential pitfalls that could hurt their finances, and current market trends for short-term rental properties in that area. Additionally, if it's possible, visit the property in person so you can get a better understanding of the location and see if there's anything that could prevent or increase profitability. It's also wise to reach out to other investors or experienced professionals who may be able to provide insight on specific opportunities they either have pursued or are familiar with. When it comes down to investing in short-term rental properties, thorough analysis and research can pay off when it comes to making money. , when investing in short-term rental properties, it is important to have a plan for dealing with potential risks. This means having a clear understanding of potential income, analyzing the costs associated with owning and running the property, and forming an appropriate strategy for collecting payments from tenants. By taking these steps into account before making any investments, investors can ensure that their short-term rental properties are as profitable as possible. In addition, having an understanding of legal regulations in the area is essential for avoiding any issues with the local government. With all this knowledge and these tips, analyzing and investing in short-term rental properties can be a lucrative decision for potential investors.

Overall, investing in short-term rental properties can be a great way to make money. However, it's essential to do your research and understand the potential risks associated with such investments. By following this advice and taking advantage of any opportunities that may arise, investors can find

success when it comes to their short-term rental

properties.

CHAPTER 5
Where Is The Best Short-Term RentaL LOCATION Market for Real Estate Investors?

For real estate investors looking for the best short-term rental location, there's no one-size-fits-all answer; it really depends on the investor's needs. Generally speaking, sunny weather, popular attractions, and nearby airport accessibility draw in desirable tenants. Coastal or mountain regions tend to have high demand due to proximity to beaches or ski resorts. For a lower price point property, look to destinations that are gaining popularity but haven't yet spiked prices; this could be an up-and-coming neighborhood or a small college town. Additionally, regions near business hubs or military bases that see frequent renter turnover may offer solid investment opportunities. With careful research of local housing markets and trends, savvy investors can find just the right short-term rental location that suits their goals.

Once the suitable location has been determined, it's time to start looking for a rental property. It's important to consider costs such as mortgage payments and insurance, estimated maintenance expenses and any potential local taxes that may apply. Prospective investors should research recent sales of similar properties in their chosen area to determine an appropriate price point. Additionally, investors can look into the type of tenant they expect to attract; is it families seeking vacation rentals or business travelers? Regardless of the target demographic, attractive amenities like high-speed internet access or a pool could help draw more renters.

Finding the right short-term rental location isn't always easy, but with proper research and due diligence, real estate investors can find just the right spot for their needs. With the right combination of pricing, amenities and location, investors can take advantage of the profitable potential of short-term rentals.

Note that the exact answer will depend on your target real estate market and budget. Here are some of the most critical

 short-**term rental markets you should keep an eye on in 2023**

Nashville, Tennessee

Chattanooga, Tennessee—located along the Tennessee River in the shadows of the Appalachian Mountains—offers a promising investment opportunity, with Zillow predicting a 17% increase in property values by 2022. The Lookout Mountain

Incline Railway transports visitors to historical structures and trails with breathtaking views.

- Potential annual revenue: $47,000

- Rating for revenue growth: 78

- The rental demand rating is 98.

- Rating for Investability: 88

- Investor rating: 88

Tennessee's Sevierville

Dolly Parton's hometown, which overlooks the majestic Smoky Mountains, can provide visitors with a once-in-a-lifetime experience. It's also a year-round favorite among great-outdoors enthusiasts.

- Potential annual revenue: $61,961

- Rating for revenue growth: 65

- Rating for rental demand: 71

- Rating for Investability: 100

- Investor rating: 83.9

Hawaii, Maui

Maui is the best Airbnb investment destination in 2022 due to high occupancy and a strong economy.

Because of its high occupancy, strong income growth from 2020, and high investability, Maui is the best Airbnb investment destination in 2022.

The Valley Isle is well-known for its world-famous beaches, humpback whale sightings, and breathtaking sunsets.

- Potential annual revenue: $102,000

- Rating for revenue growth: 90

- Rating for rental demand: 93

- Rating for Investability: 91

- Investor rating: 90

Alaska's Kenai Peninsula

The Kenai Peninsula offers access to numerous national parks, wildlife viewing opportunities, and the genuine awe and beauty of Alaska. There has been a surge in interest in outdoor adventure since the pandemic. As a result, it's not surprising that the region's revenue growth has a score of 94.

- Potential annual revenue: $44,000

- Rating for revenue growth: 94

- Rating for rental demand: 89

- Rating for Investability: 87

- Investor score. 89

Apply for licenses and permits

Common licenses and permits needed before renting your property include a general business license and a short-term rental license.

Applying for licenses and permits to rent out your property can take some time, but it's worth it to make sure you have all of your paperwork in order before beginning. Common licenses and permits that may be necessary include a general business license as well as a short-term rental license in order to legally rent out your space. Doing the proper research around local laws and regulations is also an important step for any would-be landlord; understanding what is required of you can help set expectations for your renters much more easily. Make sure you have all the appropriate documents so that when the time comes, you can confidently manage this important part of being a landlord.

Some local governments may require additional paperwork, such as zoning permits and other fees. Researching these items can help you better understand any extra costs associated with renting out your property. Additionally, some insurance policies may be required in order to cover any potential damages that could occur due to a tenant's negligence. Knowing the details of what is expected from landlords in your area can save valuable time and hassle down the road.

In short, applying for the necessary licenses and permits needed before renting out your property is an important step for all would-be landlords. Doing research around local laws and regulations, understanding what documents are necessary, and being aware of any extra fees or insurance policies that may be required can help make this process much smoother. Taking the time to get everything in order can pay off in the long run, so make sure you check all your boxes before renting out your property. Continuing from above:

Once you have all of your paperwork in order and are ready to start advertising your rental, it's time to create an effective marketing plan. Developing a thoughtful strategy around how you advertise and promote your unit is important for finding quality tenants quickly. Think about what makes your space unique and decide which methods you'll use to promote it - online listings, word-of-mouth advertising, or even local flyers or posters might be helpful depending on the area where your property is located. Additionally, think through any extra details that could help attract tenants - are you offering any special amenities or services? Listing these details in your ad can be a great way to make it stand out.

Once you've created an effective marketing plan and started advertising, applications will start coming in. Gather potential renters' contact information and review their applications closely; carefully evaluate each one before making a decision on who to accept. The process of choosing the right tenant can be daunting, so make sure you do your due diligence by verifying employment status and conducting background checks. You should also consider requiring a rental deposit and having the tenant sign a lease agreement for extra protection against things like late rent payments or damages to the property. Taking all of these steps can save time and money in the long run.

Making sure you have all of your paperwork and

marketing plans in order before renting out your

property is key for successful landlords. Take the

time to research local laws, understand what

documents are necessary, and create an effective

advertising strategy - these steps can help make

this process much easier in the long-**term.**

CHAPTER6
Determine pricing

How you price your short-term rental will have a huge impact on the success of your business. You want to be competitive, but you also need to cover your expenses (both expected and unexpected)

- Mortgage or rent

- Insurance premiums

- Business license and permit fees

- Renovation and repairs

- Listing fees

- Cleaning and laundry services

- Landscaping

- HOA fees

- Newer appliances

The next step is to assess the risks associated with the project. Risk assessment involves identifying and analyzing potential problems that could arise during the course of the project. This includes examining things like financial, technical, legal, and environmental issues that could affect the success of the project. Once all potential risks have been identified and analyzed, a strategy must be developed to mitigate them. This may include things like setting up contingency plans or insurance policies to provide protection in case of unexpected events.

Once risk assessment is completed, it's time to begin planning out how to achieve the objectives set forth in your business plan. This involves creating a detailed timeline for each stage of the project as well as assigning resources such as personnel and materials needed for successful completion. Additionally, you'll need to create a budget **that outlines the estimated costs of the project and identifies where funds will be allocated.**

Finally, it's time to put together a pricing strategy for your short-term rental. The best way to do this is by considering the cost of similar properties in your area and setting your price accordingly so that it is competitive yet still covers all expenses plus provides you with an adequate profit margin. Additionally, consider offering discounts or other incentives such as loyalty programs to help attract more customers and boost your bottom line. By taking these steps, you can ensure that your business succeeds in providing top notch services while also turning a healthy profit.

Automate your rental tasks

Because short-term rentals have a high guest turnover, look for ways to streamline property management and bookings. Online reservations, guest reviews, contactless and keyless check-in, occupancy tax remittance, payment processing, and more can make for a seamless experience for you and your guests

Automating your rental tasks can save you time and money in the short-term rental game. A few simple steps to streamline property management, bookings, guest reviews, check-ins, and payment processing can do wonders for you and your guests. With online reservations you can easily manage: tax remittance, contactless entry to the premises with a keyless system, as well as fast and secure payment processing. Automation offers an ease of experience without needing to be onsite at all times. It will also help you keep track of all the details for each booking so that you can rest easy knowing everything is taken care of.

For the guests, automation can make for an easy and hassle-free check-in. Keyless entry systems allow them to enter without having to meet anyone in person, which is especially convenient for late arrivals and those who want a higher level of privacy. Automation also allows for quick payment processing as well as automatic reviews that provide valuable insights into how your property is faring with each guest.

Overall, automation makes life easier for both you and your guests by taking out the guesswork and allowing you to focus on creating memorable experiences instead of dealing with tedious tasks. So take the time to explore automation options available to help streamline your short-term rental business today!

What Are the Legal Constraints of Short-Term Rental Regulations?

You've probably used Airbnb or other short-term rental services at some point in your life. But have you ever considered that **Airbnb is illegal in some places?**

In New York City, for example, renting out a property for less than 30 days is illegal. Despite this, NYC is one of the largest Airbnb markets, with listings available for less than 30 days. And the penalties for breaking the law are severe: putting out an illegal advertisement can result in a $7,500 fine.

Whether or not it is legal to rent out a property depends on several factors, including the location and type of property you own, as well as how long you have owned it. Regulations Vary From City to City

Many counties and cities have established legal restrictions on STRs, which can range from mild to severe (making STRs illegal in some places). Before renting out a property, hosts are usually required to register as short term renters and obtain a short term rental license. As a prospective host, you must arrange for local occupancy taxes, pay various fees, and meet insurance and other requirements.

Some municipalities may use zoning laws to limit STRs. You can operate a short-term rental property in San Luis Obispo County (CA), but it must be located within 200 feet of another similar rental.

The Isle of Palms (SC) has a two-person limit per bed, plus an additional two people.

A residential property in an apartment building (or another type of multiple residential dwelling unit) in New York City must be used solely for permanent resident purposes. In other words, the property must be occupied by the same people for 30 days in a row (or more). It is illegal to accommodate paying guests for less than 30 days unless your property is a bed-and-breakfast or licensed hotel.

Milwaukee, Memphis, Philadelphia, Phoenix, Atlanta, Dallas, Tampa, and Cleveland are among the cities with the most relaxed short-term rental policies (to name a few). They are the places with little to no Airbnb and short term rental issues because they have a short term rental license and a low occupancy tax rate.

Tampa, FL is one of the best cities in the United States for short-term rentals.

Tampa FL is one of the US cities with the most lax vacation rental rules, making a short term rental license application relatively simple.

What Permits Are Required to Operate a Short-Term Rental?

Everything is subject to your city or county's short-term rental regulations. Still, obtaining a general business license and a short-term rental license is frequently required.

For any type of business, a general business license is required. It is a basic license required for conducting business with your local jurisdiction. Make sure your short-term rental business is registered with your local government. If your county or city does not have a business licensing department, you can obtain the information from your local tax office.

Given the restrictions and regulations we've discussed, you'll almost certainly need a short-term rental license. The permit will assist you in complying with zoning restrictions, ensuring that your short-term rental meets property safety and health requirements, and notifying all neighboring properties. Your licensing department may request proof that the property you intend to rent is not your primary residence.

You should also pay attention and gather all relevant taxation information. There is no consistent tax policy for Airbnb renters, and tax policies vary by city. Learn everything you can about your local laws in order to determine what you will need to pay or collect in order to host. You may also need to apply for a tax identification number. You'd like to rent it out. Furthermore, legal restrictions on STRs can be perplexing and inconsistent.

CHAPTER 7

7 Best Cities in the United States for Short-Term Rentals

Pleasant weather, ample living space, and reasonable rent are all factors that influence people's decisions when looking for the ideal rental property. We used fresh and accurate data from Airbnb, MLS, and other private and public records to help you find the best cities for real estate investors. Some cities have excellent short-term and long-term rental potential, but if the STR regulations are too complex and restrictive, Airbnb long-term rentals may be your best bet.

So, before you start looking for the right investment property and getting your short-term rental license, let's go over some of the best places to start.

Columbus, Ohio

Airbnb Columbus Ohio owners could rent out their property without a permit until 2019. However, the city has since required a permit, which you can learn about and obtain through its Licensing Section.

Property owners who leased five or fewer units for less than 30 consecutive days were already required to obtain a permit in order to operate. The 2019 ordinance modifies a few sections of the Columbus Code that govern short-term and hotel/motel rental operations, as well as the permitting process (Chapter 598).

The ordinance added new grounds for permit revocation, denial, or suspension. It also includes new procedures for objecting, notifying, and appealing, as well as more information on permit requirements.

Let's look at the numbers for the Airbnb Columbus Ohio rental market to help you with your Airbnb analysis:

- $2,263 in Airbnb rental income

- Airbnb's cash-on-cash return is 24%.

- The daily rate for Airbnb is $130.

- 57% of Airbnb listings are occupied.

- The average home costs $378,086.

- Days on Market: 82 Average Price per Square Foot: $232

- Score for walking: 41

You can get your short-term rental license at the Department of Public Safety License Section, which is located at 4252 Grove Rd. The permit for your non-primary residence will cost you $150 per calendar year, and the permit for your primary residence will cost you $75. You must hand in your signed short-term rental application and pay a $20 fee in person.

2. The city of Washington, D.C.

In Washington, DC, they began enforcing a three-year-old law that regulates and limits online short-term rentals. It now requires hosts to obtain permits and limits the amount of time they can rent out their home or apartment each year. The law was passed by the local council in 2018, but it was not implemented until January 2022.

The law specifically applies to Airbnb Washington DC businesses and other short-term rentals lasting less than 30 days. You must obtain a short-term rental license from the Department of Consumer and Regulatory Affairs if you want to rent out an entire home, bedroom, or basement on Airbnb (DCRA).

You can host short-term renters for as long as you want over the course of a year if you (the owner) are present in the property during the rental. It is ideal for those who, for example, rent out their basement or engage in rental arbitrage while remaining in the property. However, if you are not present, your rentals are restricted to a total of 90 days per year. In addition, you will be unable to obtain a short-term rental license for your second home.

Take a look at the numbers below before deciding to start your Airbnb Washington DC business and apply for a license:

- $2,959 in Airbnb rental income

- Airbnb's cash-on-cash return is 87%.

- The daily rate for Airbnb is $149.

- 63% of Airbnb listings are occupied.

- The average home costs $724,631.

- The average cost per square foot is
  $642.

- 115 days on the market

- Score for walking: 61

With a high number of both Airbnb (3,217) and traditional (4,777) listings, we can say that DC is currently a strong buyer's market. The short term rental market is also active, so purchasing a short term investment property here would be a wise decision. Due to the intense competition, make sure to nail your marketing and set the right pricing.

3. Seattle, Washington

To become an Airbnb Seattle host, you must first apply for a license through the City of Seattle website. The Department of Finance and Administrative Services will issue you a short-term rental license for $75 per unit. Once you have your license, you must include the number and expiration date in your Airbnb listings. Licenses are valid for 12 months, and when they expire, you will receive an email with a renewal reminder. Your license can be renewed through your Seattle Services Portal account.

You may operate up to two of your own dwelling units as short-term rentals. One must be your primary residence, and the other may be any property you own (such as a second home or vacation home).

Do you want to start an Airbnb Seattle project and conduct an Airbnb analysis? Here is some new information to help you plan your finances:

Rental income from Airbnb: $3,320

- Airbnb's cash-on-cash return is 8%.

- Airbnb's daily rate is $153.

- 69% of Airbnb listings are occupied.

- The average home costs $584,958.

- The average cost per square foot is $618.

- 63 days on the market

- Score for walking: 68

Related: Finding Investment Property in Seattle's Real Estate Market

Denver, Colorado

Many people in Denver choose to engage in rental arbitrage because it allows them to rent out more than their primary residence.

The Denver City Council mandated in 2016 that any property owner who wants to start a short term rental business obtain a Denver short term rental license. The rental must be your primary residence, and you must follow all insurance, zoning, and safety regulations. Failure to comply with the requirements for Airbnb Denver rentals may result in a $1,000 fine per transaction.

You can apply for a short-term rental license in Denver through the city's Online Permitting and Licensing Center. Open the

Business, Short-Term Rental, and Occupational Licensing page, click Apply New, and then choose the license type you want.

Let's look at the most recent Airbnb Denver statistics. Profit projections can be made using your budget and the following data:

- Rental income from Airbnb: $3,540

- Airbnb's cash-on-cash return is 49%.

- The daily rate for Airbnb is $172.

- 71% of Airbnb listings are occupied.

- The average home costs $535,549 dollars.

- Days on Market: 56 Average Price per Square Foot: $2,120

- Score for walking: 57

However, because Denver is one of the top ten most populated cities, it may be a better fit for Airbnb long-term rentals. Short term rentals necessitate the acquisition of a license and the purchase of additional investment properties in order to convert them to short term rentals.

The monthly traditional rental income ($2,264) is less than the Airbnb rental income, but it's still a good side income.

You won't have to communicate with many guests, be available 24 hours a day, make quality assurances, manage cleaners, or spend a lot of time managing your rental.

Austin, Texas

Austin's short-term rental ordinance distinguishes three types of properties:

Single-family or duplex homes (not owner-occupied)

Multifamily housing (not owner-occupied)

Property types include single-family homes, multifamily homes, and duplexes (owner-occupied)

If you want to start your Airbnb Austin business, you'll need a short-term rental license for each of them. The ordinance places the most restrictions on non-owner-occupied single-family and duplex properties. They are restricted to commercially zoned town areas (such as Downtown Mixed Use (DMU) and Central Business District (CBD) areas).

The Airbnb Austin numbers listed below should help you understand how to invest in rental properties in Austin and develop your rental strategy:

- Rental income from Airbnb: $3,735

- Airbnb's cash-on-cash return is 45%.

- Airbnb's daily rate is $237.

- 58% of Airbnb listings are occupied.

- The average home costs $700,189.

- The average cost per square foot is $445.

- 66 days on the market

- Score for walking: 50

Austin, on the other hand, is solidifying itself as a tech hub on par with other major tech cities, thanks to an increasing number of technology companies in the city. Add to that its affordability in comparison to the cost of living in California's major cities, and it's no surprise that many people are flocking to Austin for work. Investing in long-term rentals may be a better option here.

New Orleans, Louisiana

Anyone interested in hosting short-term stays on Airbnb in New Orleans must obtain an owner and operator STR license. But first, you must determine which type of license you are eligible for. Following that, you can apply for your license through the city's website.

You can also download the application forms, fill them out, and email them back. Homeowners can rent out entire houses or rooms for up to 30 days in a row if they pay a $150 short-term rental license fee, apply for an annual license, and collect city taxes from guests.

Before you start looking for an Airbnb for sale, take a look at the Airbnb New Orleans data below.

- Airbnb Rental Earnings: $3,268

- Airbnb's cash-on-cash return is 66%.

- Airbnb's daily rate is $204.

- 58% of Airbnb listings are occupied.

- The average home costs $546,176.

- The average cost per square foot is $333.

- 72 days on the market

- Score for walking: 56 7.

Atlanta, Georgia

Airbnb Atlanta renters must apply to the DPCD for a short-term rental license (Department of Planning and Community Development). The application fee of $150 is non-refundable.An owner or long-term tenant may license their property to an agent under the city's new ordinance (who can be another person or themselves). They can obtain a short-term rental license for their primary residence as well as one additional property. Every year, the license must be renewed.

Here are some recent data points to assist Airbnb Atlanta renters in developing the best renting strategy:

- $2,267 in Airbnb rental income

- Airbnb's cash-on-cash return is 1.03%.

- Airbnb daily rate is $156; occupancy rate is 46%.

- The average home costs $568,865.

- Days on Market: 81 Average Price per Square Foot: $1,168

- Score for walking: 43

More importantly, automation offers a layer of security against potential liabilities. With automated property management systems, you can know that all of the details are taken care of, from safety and occupancy requirements to taxes and payments. This gives you peace of mind that no matter who checks in or out, everything is accounted for and up to date. Automation also allows for better tracking and communication throughout the process with automatic messages sent out when certain actions occur. This helps ensure everyone is on the same page with booking timelines, payment procedures, check-in rules, reviews and more. Finally, automation makes it easier to manage multiple properties at once by giving an overview of occupancy across all properties in one place. This way, you can quickly see where each property is at and make necessary adjustments if needed.

In short, automating your rental tasks can help make for a smoother process for both you and your guests. With automation, you don't have to worry about tedious tasks like bookings, payments or occupancy requirements – it's all taken care of! So take the time to explore the automation options available and streamline your rental business today.

Finally, automation helps foster long-term relationships with customers by making them feel secure. Automation allows them to quickly book, review and pay without needing to jump through any hoops. The less hassle, the more likely they are to book again in the future and your property will get repeat business! Additionally, automated reviews provide useful information on how customers view your property. This feedback is invaluable and can be used to improve customer service or make changes based on what guests enjoy or what could use improvement. In conclusion, automation can help you save time and money while also creating a better experience for both you and your guests in the short-term rental market. With online reservations, keyless entry systems, payment processing solutions, occupancy tracking, and automatic reviews, you can ensure all of the details are taken care of so that you can focus on creating memorable experiences for everyone involved. Automation makes it easier to manage multiple properties and foster long-term relationships with customers, so take the time to explore the automation options available today!

REFERENCES

Mashvisor Tools Archives | Mashvisor

Short-Term Rentals - Business Regulations |
seattle.gov

Bookiply - More bookings for your vacation rental

§ 117.02 SHORT TERM RENTAL BUSINESS LICENSES.
(amlegal.com)

Printed by BoD™ in Norderstedt, Germany